# The Art & History of Whiteknights

Jenny Halstead studied Art and Design at Sutton and Cheam School of Art, followed by a Guest Scholarship at the Royal Academy Schools. She then trained and worked as a medical artist and natural history illustrator, working on many publications including several editions of *Gray's Anatomy,* a book *Bare Bones* – an exploration of art and science – and a series of children's books on dinosaurs, before moving on into her own work and a wider spectrum.

This turning point coincided with the setting up of Whiteknights Studio Trail in 2000. She has been an exhibitor since the beginning and the coordinator for 15 years. She has published two books with Two Rivers Press: *An Artist's Year in the Harris Garden* and *Silchester: Life on the Dig.*

Also published by Two Rivers Press

*The Art of Peter Hay* by John Froy with Martin Andrews
*Bonjour Mr Inshaw* by Peter Robinson & David Inshaw
*Botanical Artistry* by Julia Trickey
*The Greenwood Trees: History, folklore and uses of Britain's trees* by Christina Hart-Davies
*Reading Abbey and the Abbey Quarter* by Peter Durrant and John Painter
*Reading's Bayeux Tapestry* by Reading Museum
*A Coming of Age: Celebrating 18 Years of Botanical Painting by the Eden Project Florilegium Society*
    by Ros Franklin
*A Wild Plant Year: History, folklore and uses of Britain's flora* by Christina Hart-Davies
*Silchester: Life on the Dig* by Jenny Halstead & Michael Fulford
*Caught on Camera: Reading in the 70s* by Terry Allsop
*Plant Portraits by Post: Post & Go British Flora* by Julia Trickey
*Allen W. Seaby: Art and Nature* by Martin Andrews & Robert Gillmor
*Cover Birds* by Robert Gillmor
*An Artist's Year in the Harris Garden* by Jenny Halstead
*Caversham Court Gardens: A Heritage Guide* by Friends of Caversham Court Gardens
*Birds, Blocks & Stamps: Post & Go Birds of Britain* by Robert Gillmor
*Down by the River: The Thames and Kennet in Reading* by Gillian Clark

# The Art & History of Whiteknights

Edited by Jenny Halstead

First published in the UK in 2020 by Two Rivers Press
7 Denmark Road, Reading RG1 5PA.
www.tworiverspress.com

ISBN 978-1-909747-61-6

1 2 3 4 5 6 7 8 9

Two Rivers Press is represented in the UK by Inpress Ltd and distributed
by NBNi.

Cover design and lettering by Sally Castle
Typeset in Parisine

Printed and bound in Great Britain by Gomer Press, Ceredigion

FSC
www.fsc.org
MIX
Paper from
responsible sources
FSC® C114687

## Acknowledgements

Whiteknights Studio Trail and Two Rivers Press are extremely
grateful to The Claydon Family Trust, RG Spaces and The Friends
of the University of Reading for their generous financial support
of this project.

## Picture credits

With thanks to the following for permission to reproduce
   the photographs:
Reading Local Studies Library (p.v and p.31)
Fiona Talkington (p.vi; top right)
Paul & Rupert Peskett (p.vi; bottom left)
Salvo Toscano (p.vi; bottom right)
Evelyn Williams (p.30)
The Museum of English Rural Life, University of Reading,
Dann-Lewis Photographic Collection (p.32, p.36, p.37).
And an unknown benefactor who gave Jenny the old photograph
   of Christchurch Green (p.vi; top left).

ADMISSION TO WHITEKNIGHTS.

BY PERMISSION OF THE

PROPRIETORS.

No.    [Not Transferable.

No admission
without a ticket.    GEORGE LOVEJOY.

Admission from Two o'clock; Close at Nine.

∗₊∗ It is expected that all Persons will protect the
Plants, &c, from Injury.

A season ticket for entry to Whiteknights Park, c.1860s,
which allowed the public access to enjoy the delights of the
landscape and lake. This ticket belonged to George Lovejoy
(1808–1883), who ran the biggest subscription library in the
South of England. His premises in London Street were next
to what is now the Great Expectations Hotel and the buildings
have changed very little from his day. The labyrinth of twisty
staircases and rooms stacked with books were visited by many
of the literary figures of the day including Charles Dickens,
William Makepeace Thackeray, Algernon Charles Swinburne,
Anthony Trollope and Lovejoy's great friend, Mary Russell
Mitford.

# Contents

Christchurch Green

# Foreword

As I write this, on a cold December day, I hear cars and buses idling at the traffic lights, the piercing notes of an ambulance siren, people shouting on their phones, drilling from nearby roadworks. Was it really so long ago that the clip-clop of a horse's hooves was part of the soundtrack to this area, as it pulled the baker's van delivering bread? I was born near Christchurch Green, and this has been my family home ever since. There were no traffic lights, the Green itself was a different shape, my school (St Joseph's) was at the corner of Northcourt Avenue and cows grazed on the Whiteknights Campus. I cried when the flint cottages nearby were knocked down. My mother took me to buy broken biscuits at Teetgens; Miss Godfrey at the haberdasher's was a formidable lady selling lace and knicker elastic. I can still smell the sawdust on the butcher's floor, and, at the greengrocer's, Mr and Mrs Franklin gave me bananas. I had my first Saturday job in Budgens (the successor to Teetgens, and which eventually became the Devana restaurant); I walked around Whiteknights chatting with school friends and I learned my love of prog rock from neighbours in New Road. I grew up and, later, my own children took their new bikes onto campus, walked to school, learned to cross the roads (now with traffic lights) and were given bananas by Mrs Franklin.

There's something about the Whiteknights area that makes people stay here. The University and the Royal Berks Hospital help to define us, bringing staff and students, a diverse community with languages and skills from around the world. The chants of the students' Bonfire Night parades, or Rag Day, may have disappeared, but we chat at the bus stops with students from China, Iran or Serbia and we are richer for it. We are comforted in the hospital by staff from so many countries and we learn deep human connections.

It's not surprising that the Whiteknights Studio Trail has grown out of this wonderful creative community and established itself as part of the lifeblood of this very special town of ours. The passion of Jenny Halstead and her co-founders is remarkable. Because of them we walk around the area every June, feeling our own creativity enhanced by the exhibitors who so generously open their houses, and we marvel at the brickwork, the gardens, their inspiration and talent.

Twenty years of the Whiteknights Studio Trail is a fantastic achievement. It's an opportunity to celebrate the history and heritage of this area with the inspirational artwork in these pages. Thank you for allowing me to be a little nostalgic too, and remember once more the hot breath of the baker's horse on my hand as I hold out an apple.

Congratulations WST! Here's to the next 20 years!

*Fiona Talkington*
*Reading, December 2019*

Fiona Talkington has been a presenter for BBC Radio 3 for 30 years and is a proud Reading resident!

# The Whiteknights Studio Trail

## A celebration of our 20th year

It was the summer of the new millennium when three local artists – Susanna Beer (weaver), Pip Hall (stone-carver) and Jenny Halstead (painter) – met to formulate an idea and fulfil a passion – a studio trail around the area of Whiteknights campus.

We shared a concern about the lack of exhibiting space in Reading and the belief that there were enough creative artists and crafts-people in this area to form a walking tour from one studio venue to the next. The idea was, and still is, to make it a community event, with exhibitors displaying their work and communicating their enthusiasm and the processes of their craft to visitors.

A single summer weekend was agreed, with all venues open on both days. That December, we arranged a meeting and invited interested artists (mainly professional) living in the area who were keen to be part of the event and pay a subscription.

2001: On 23 & 24 June the first WST took place, with a simple single-colour brochure and a printed booklet about the artists sponsored by Southern Arts. It was an amazing success for everyone involved, exhibitors and visitors alike.

We then started to talk about a future, with a change of roles. Susanna and Jenny stepped down as Secretary and Treasurer and Vivienne Loren (not a participant), replaced Pip as Chair and fundraiser and was elected Chairperson and Coordinator.

2003: We had a WST Constitution with Aims and Objectives and an AGM. We introduced selection to maintain standards with a Selection Committee and established working as a cooperative.

2004: I became WST Coordinator as well as an exhibitor and have remained so to date.

2005: Our website – www.studiotrail.co.uk – was launched and we adopted our WST logo.

Since then we have grown and flourished but are always mindful to remain contained within the area as a walking tour, with guest exhibitors applying annually to keep it vibrant and fresh.

2010: On our 10th anniversary we were granted extra funding and had an extended brochure that included 55 artists, the Ridgeline Trust, RFT, Music@Reading and for the first time the Fine Art Degree Show.

2017: We celebrated the 70th anniversary of the Reading–Düsseldorf twinning by inviting two artists from Düsseldorf to come to Reading and exhibit with us.

2019: We created a new category 'WST Introduces...' inviting young artists (aged 18–22) to show with us free of charge.

WST Comes to Town: On four occasions we have arranged an extra pop-up winter show in the centre of Reading in Gun Street, Kings Arcade, Haslams and HolyBrook Gallery.

The University of Reading has offered us sponsorship since 2005 and other bodies and individuals have supported us over the years, for which we are extremely grateful. Over these 20 years this has enabled us to welcome around 200 artists and curate some 650 exhibitions in studios and mixed venues in this local community, the area of Whiteknights.

*Jenny Halstead*

# Ursula Waechter

**Lettered Plate**
Tin-glazed earthenware, 235 mm diameter

Over the last 10 years I have enjoyed being part of the Whiteknights Trail as a guest artist.

Part of my practice is producing commissioned lettered pieces to celebrate special occasions such as christenings, weddings and anniversaries, so it seemed a natural choice to produce a commemorative plate for the Studio Trail.

I work in tin-glazed earthenware, which traditionally has been used for this kind of work. The plate is thrown on the potter's wheel and turned at leather-hard stage to shape the foot, dried completely and biscuit-fired. The glaze is applied by dipping. I work out the size of the lettering and the design on paper to suit the plate and paint the lettering and design using differently shaped and sized brushes with oxide mixtures on the unfired glaze. After this the plate is glaze-fired.

I have used a muted blue and warm orange as the key colours, which to me epitomise the feeling of the Trail as reflected in the annual leaflets.

# Carole Stephens

## Monster Teapot at MERL
### Mixed media

Why choose the teapot from MERL? First of all, it's enormous, made by Michael Cardew in c.1938, with an ironwork stand by a local black-smith, Mr Bayliss. I love teapots, so what better example than this 'country' ware typical of so many things on display at the Museum of English Rural Life? I've changed colour and background to reflect my own interest in pattern and decoration.

At MERL in 2017, Sam Knight and I had the pleasure of sharing the WST venue with two art-ists from Düsseldorf, our twin town. A challenge to perceived Whiteknights Studio Trail style, but altogether a delightful experience, artistically and socially.

WST is always a happy event. Friends come, buyers from previous years drop in to see how your work is evolving or changing, and people new to it ask of the work, 'How do you do it?' It feels as if the sun is always shining.

Why the teapot? Tea and cake are simply an essential part of the Whiteknights Studio Trail.

# Tom Cartmill

Collect. A Coming Together
Ink on paper

I have had the pleasure of showing my art during Whiteknights Studio Trail, in the beautiful Peckover Hall at Leighton Park, for over 10 years.

I usually exhibit in what is now a classroom, but the stuccoed ceiling arches, oak-panelled walls and imposing fireplace hint at its original use as a library. I have been most fortunate to be able to display my art there, in such a well-proportioned and sympathetic space. 'Peckover', as everyone calls it, was designed by the Quaker architects Thorp and Rowntree for Reading's, and indeed Berkshire's, only Quaker school.

The title of my drawing refers to not only the yearly influx of artists and Studio Trail visitors during the WST weekend, but also to the Quaker tradition of 'collect', where everyone in the school community comes together in the hall on a daily basis, sitting and observing a silence. A convention that, most agree, instils the school with a unique atmosphere.

# Sue Mundy

Whiteknights Woods – 'Whiteknights Lignums'
Ceramic – black stoneware

Having grown up around the Whiteknights area I have walked through these woods many, many times. Either with my family as a young child, hearing stories from my mother of skating on the lake, or as a teenager with friends looking for a place to hang out. These trees have played their part throughout my life.

Today I come back to this special place, which never fails to inspire and excite me. As a professional ceramic maker, I look to the natural world to inform my practice. My love is trees, especially in winter when the bare carcass of the tree body is revealed. Whiteknights has a particularly wonderful selection of diverse tree species with many different colours, textures and patterns.

A magical place within the busy urban world.

# Jenny Halstead

Christchurch Green – Autumn
Oil on canvas

I have lived in the Whiteknights area of Reading for over 35 years. My house was built around 1790 and was originally a farmhouse. The cottages alongside are the same period and were all surrounded by farmland and fields. Christchurch Green, a few yards away, graced with various trees including an apple, has changed its shape over the years and was situated close to the site of the old Toll Gate at the top of Redlands Road (then Red Lane).

I have welcomed thousands of WST visitors to my studio over the last 20 years – it was originally the dairy with a sluice down the centre of the floor. The parade of shops opposite the house has changed considerably over the years. It first comprised a hardware store, greengrocer, Post Office, a laundry, an off-licence, two banks, a butcher, a baker but alas no candlestick maker!

This is still a busy community, which nevertheless retains its 'village' feel in spite of a large and ever-changing student population.

# Chris Mercier

Studio 4, TOB1 – No. 1 Earley Gate (2019)
Screen print

At Earley Gate, Whiteknights Campus, stands a series of 1940s pre-fabs built by the MOD, some of which were used as a military hospital. They were decommissioned and acquired by the University of Reading in 1965 – 9.

As a child in the 1960s, cycling through the campus, I remember being spooked by heaps of discarded prosthetic limbs stacked up in the yard of TOB1, which by then was used as a maintenance store. A stone's throw away and still standing was The Citadel, (Region 6 War Room and nuclear bunker).

In 1989 The Fine Art Department, headed by Martin Froy, moved from London Road to TOB1. The students contested the move and lobbied the Vice-Chancellor, Ewan Page, taking their protest to the steps of the National Gallery. The Director, Neil MacGregor, was a former lecturer in History of Art at Reading. The VC, as a gesture of appeasement, saw that a large studio with north-facing skylights was built ready for the 1990 Degree Show.

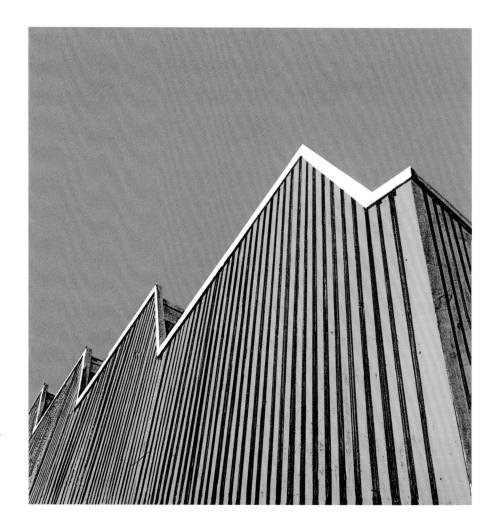

# Sam Knight

## Upper Redlands Road
Digital collage of hand-painted paper

Walking around the Whiteknights area evokes memories of my childhood as the Studio Trail was always a prominent part of my summer. My mother and I would walk the trail together when I was young and I continued to do so throughout my teenage years. Now, as an adult, I enjoy returning to Reading to participate in the Studio Trail as an artist.

The brickwork around Upper Redlands Road and the surrounding area has always been of interest to me. The bricks are weathered and worn, yet beautifully decorative, serving as a visual representation of Reading and its history.

I have chosen to respond to the colours, textures and weathering of the brickwork as this reflects my ongoing artistic projects on road surfaces and markings, subjects I intend to explore further. I created surfaces using a range of media including inks, acrylics and spray paint, which I then photographed and assembled into a digital collage.

# Natasha Zavialov

Flying Above the Park
Mixed media on paper

For ten years I walked my children to school. Our favoured route went through the University park; it was pleasant at any time of the year. I have memories of ducks scrambling over the first ice on the lake, shady green tunnels made of shrubbery, and fish swimming in the shallows. It was a place where you could always find quiet, peace and happiness.

# Celeste Kelly

Foxhill House
Oil on board

When I first moved into the Whiteknights area almost six years ago I knew very few people here. It wasn't long before local residents welcomed me to my new home and a kind neighbour even left some scones on my doorstep.

In the early days I would walk around the University grounds and lake with my little dog Walter; there we came across the back of Foxhill House looking out towards the lake. A tall, red-brick, gothic-revival-style building with bright-red painted window frames, a white veranda with hedges in front of it and vivid green grass rolling down towards the water. Over time the house has become a friend, as has this area and its people, so it seemed fitting that I would do a painting of it.

Foxhill was built in 1868 by the architect Alfred Waterhouse and was used as his own residence until the early 1870s, when he moved to Yattendon Court. It is also a Grade II listed building.

# Trevor Powell

Whiteknights Lake
Oil painting

The Whiteknights lake has been a part of my life for well over 30 years: for running, then jogging, and then walking the dog in the early morning half-light. I've gradually moved closer – living in five houses in the area – and now live within 150 metres. The trees on the bank provide strong, dark, vertical and diagonal lines, leaning and dipping their branches into the water; swathes of greens, browns and oranges and then the pool of water – not blue as in my painting, but blue in my mind. The English abstract landscape painter, Ivon Hitchens, talked about 'creating a sense of place'; his use of broad brush strokes, with the white of the canvas peeping through, allowing the painting to breathe. The path around the University lake is not tarmacked, is wet with mulchy leaves in winter, and there are no benches; it is a place to move not to sit, for students, the local community, geese and wildlife.

# Rukshi Brownlow

Many Walks
Digital media

For many years I used to walk with my children through the University parkland to school. They are the happiest memories. It always surprises me every time I go, how quiet and secluded a spot we have in the middle of Reading. A jewel made brighter by all the wonderful memories it holds. It holds your hand, like an old friend, and takes you through all the seasons and years and the feeling never changes.

I have been working as a mixed media artist in this area for the last 17 years.

My work evolves and changes every year. I have created huge pieces in digital media, worked with paint, collage and printmaking. Each year brings a surprising departure and a fresh perspective. But to capture a fragment of a fleeting moment on camera is something I return to constantly. It provides the foundation on which my creativity rests.

# Elizabeth Heydeman

Garden View
Oil on canvas

This painting of my home in Northcourt Avenue contrasts the colourful comfort of woven materials with a spacious garden and distant hills beyond, seen through an Arts & Crafts window. I and fellow artists have used my home as a Whiteknights Studio Trail venue from 2001.

Coming to the University of Reading in 1957, I lodged in Northcourt Avenue, so different from the flat landscape of my home in Cambridge, excitingly on the edge of a hill with views to the west. Here the lime trees and large gardens gave it the charm of the Garden City Movement.

In 1973 I moved to one of the 1906 houses, on the west side of Northcourt Avenue, where I still live and weave. *Northcourt Avenue: its History and People (1996),* written by Penny Kemp, was published by NARA and illustrated by artists in the Avenue. Best known is Robert Gillmor, grandson of an earlier resident, Allen Seaby, Professor of Fine Art and co-founder of the Reading Guild of Artists (RGA), established in 1930.

# Thérèse Lawlor

Moonlit Visitor at Reading School
Mixed media

The lights of Reading School in the evening are an important landmark in the Whiteknights area and are always a pleasure to paint. It's even better when it snows. It doesn't happen often, but it's magical when it does. Sometimes on winter nights I can be lucky enough to see foxes saunter across the playing fields of the school. Their orange colouring really stands out against the cool tones of the snow. The foxes don't appear to be in any rush and don't seem to mind lights from the school, or passers-by on Erleigh Road.

Staff and parents are a friendly bunch at the Alfred Waterhouse-designed Reading School (chartered by King Henry VII in 1486) and allowed some of us local artists to come for a *plein air* painting session one September before the boys returned to school for autumn term. These sketches inspired me to do a wintry school scene.

# Hilary James

### Talfourd Avenue Tug-o-War
iPad

As a musician as well as an artist, I can think of nothing better than to laugh, draw, sing and play music with friends. The first Talfourd Avenue street party in 2009 was held on the Whiteknights Road allotments for the 'Big Eat'. It moved in 2012 to the street itself, where residents (and at least one former resident!) celebrated Her Maj's soggy 60th Jubilee. Children grabbed macs, bi-cycles and skipping ropes. Parents ate, drank and made merry under gazebos and umbrellas. The Talfourd social calendar has since exploded but, rain or shine, the highlight of the year is the street party!

*In memory of Andrew Clark, who started it all.*

# Susanna Beer

Donnington Gardens Weaving Studio
Weaver

The image shows part of the workspace in my house, hub of my weaving activities and site of successive Studio Trails, earning the moniker 'Aladdin's Cave'.

I have lived and worked in the Whiteknights area since my student days in 1951. My weaving began in 1990 on returning from a series of travels in New Mexico where, attending a craft school, I encountered artists who encouraged me to embark on this new project. Returning there in 1999, a knitter friend introduced me to her regional Studio Trail, which then inspired me to approach my friends Jenny and Pip to discuss initiating a similar scheme in our area; and so, in 2000, Whiteknights Studio Trail was born.

My weaving had been influenced by the powerful impact of vistas seen on my travels: the scale, contours, colours and textures, which initially led to designs for rugs woven on a floor loom, developing into more idiosyncratic wall-hangings, some with appendages of stone, metal or fibres.

# Anne-Marie Carroll

Radical
Photograph

I am lucky to have lived in the Whiteknights area of Reading for 20 years and experienced it from various viewpoints and points of view. Under-employed at times and over-employed at others but always someone who is grateful to have this area open to me so that I can be open to it. From large vistas to small cameos, there is so much to observe and to become fascinated in.

The WST is a pleasure to be part of; knowing that art is at the heart of so many people's lives here and that that life is part of the Whiteknights community is a gift.

# John Peacock

Fungi Form
Porcelain

In 1981 we moved to Earley and our two young, energetic and inquisitive sons found the woods, lakes and open spaces of Whiteknights Park a joy to explore. They played hide and seek, collected conkers and cones, spotted their first jay and green woodpeckers there and became very competitive playing Pooh sticks at the bridge. However, warily examining the wide variety of fungi with sticks really sparked their curiosity and interest and mine too. As an art teacher, I became fascinated and intrigued by the delicate structures and textures of the fungi and I soon used these features in natural form projects at Maiden Erlegh School. Later, one son completed his Typography degree at the University and our other son was based there in the 'Lego building' for his MSc. Now, as parents themselves, they bring their children to enjoy the park and as grandparents, we have been introduced to the complicated searches for geocaches and not fungi! Whiteknights has a very special place in our family life.

# Salvo Toscano

Perception of Places
Photography, black and white medium
format film (6 x 6)

How do you describe a place? Is a photo a representation of a real place or of something that
does not exist? The Whiteknights campus lake
might be said to be part of the urban fabric of
Reading – it is in the town, but at the same time it
is not, open to everybody but secluded. In captu-
ring an element of Whiteknights, I aimed to not
look for extraordinary images but for a depiction
of somewhere that is mundane and reachable:
a space that is visible but concealed as well. By
using a slow shutter approach, I sought to capture
a feeling, a perception of a place in a way it would
not be normally visible to us. For a brief moment
it is taken outside its real context.

I decided to use a black and white film to em-
phasise the mood of semi-real scenery and perceived nostalgia for a place that, as a matter of
fact, is very real and present.

# Alice Mars

Bloom
Fabric, machine and hand embroidery,
appliqué, oil markers

The Harris Garden is a treasure in Reading; an oasis nestled between busy roads in the Whiteknights area on a vast university campus, sitting quietly and beautifully, often unknown to people who have lived in Reading their entire lives. Living locally to the gardens, I visit regularly. Sometimes no one else is visiting and I have the feeling of indulging in a sanctuary just for me; sometimes it is alive with people seeking out somewhere beautiful to walk, play, romance or rest. Now with three young children in tow, it has become a favourite family haunt: somewhere to gather leaves and cones, marvel at colourful flowers, stumble across magical toadstools, climb magnificent trees, picnic in the conifer circle. It feels a world away from life around it, a place to pause and escape for just a little while, to feel connected to nature and the seasons, a joy at any time of the year.

# Joan McQuillan

Summer Meadow – The Harris Garden
Stitched textile on paper and fabric

This small botanic garden is the jewel in the campus of the University of Reading. Tucked away in a quiet corner, it is a truly relaxing haven of peace and calm, with its collection of exquisite gems of magical mini gardens.

My family have visited this incredible space over the past 40 years and watched the changes made that have added to its beauty. Despite having a large garden of our own on Shinfield Road, the Harris Garden has continually been an amazing place to visit regularly to watch the plants develop and grow.

Over the year the seasons bring their own special delights, whether it's colour, exotic blooms, or magnificent spectacles to entice and feed your imagination. The Harris Garden is truly a very special place to add to your wish list of visits and is open daily with free entry. For all these reasons, this is my most favourite place to visit time and time again.

# Cathy Newell Price

Whiteknights Brooch
Silver, precious metals, garnet, 70 × 40 mm

The shape of the Whiteknights Brooch is the out-line of the University campus (orientated with Whiteknights Road at the base). The dots indicate the perimeter of the campus – also my running route – and the little arrows show the pedestrian footpath entries. For the last 30 years I have lived within a short distance of the campus and its many footpaths have given access to the beauti-ful wildlife that can be found there. The scene of the brooch is inspired by a walk along the path that runs around the lake (from the perspective of the part adjacent to Whiteknights Road); it depicts the rushes and reeds there, with the lake and the rest of the campus beyond. I chose a garnet for the stone to symbolise the University colours. Whiteknights Studio Trail would not be so named without the Whiteknights campus and the University; that is why I chose it as my subject.

# Martin Andrews

The Old Dairy
Acrylic and ink on paper

As a member of staff at the University I have passed along Upper Redlands Road for many years on my way home and have always been intrigued by the delightful cluster of Victorian buildings on the corner with Elmhurst Road. They were originally part of the Elmhurst estate and were used to house the horses and carriages for the main house (or possibly for Park House). Around 1925 the buildings were occupied by a dairy run by Frank Pym; he delivered milk with a horse and cart to the local residents until 1942 when another milkman, Harry Pidgeon, took over the business until the late 1960s. When they became part of the University campus the buildings were used by the Museum of English Rural Life to store large farm vehicles.

I decided to take a figurative, topographical approach to my painting – exploring the texture of building materials – from a viewpoint seen by pedestrians passing by.

# Cath Baldwin

The Old Dairy – Hatherley Road
Silkscreen print

When we moved into The Redlands Dairy it had been run as a tennis racquet repair shop for some years; it was only when we began to get to know some of our neighbours and other locals that we began to understand the house we had purchased. It had been purpose-built as a shop in the 1880s and for many years sold groceries and other produce, as evidenced by the Huntley & Palmers advert in the top of the front window. More importantly, until the 1970s the shop had also offered milk deliveries, which began to explain some of the outbuildings at the back of the house – the milkman had stabled his horse in the building at the end of the garden with his cart stored in the arch to the right of the front door. We were told that 'bottling up' took place in the cellar, along with cold storage. We were also told that the milk had come from the University's own herd, but I never managed to confirm this… and it was a long time before the bell rang on a Saturday morning without us finding some poor soul clutching a broken racquet!

# Sally Castle

## The House Where I Was Born
Digital

My illustration is about memories of my birthplace, 27 Hatherley Road (front bedroom). Now it's a student house, double glazed, loft converted, wheelie bins overflowing.

We moved up to London but often visited my grandparents and great grandmother, who lived opposite at number 30. One of my treats was to go and get milk from Redlands Dairy but the best was to go to Grandad's workshop, where I would use his brace to make 'mouse holes' in a chunk of wood. The brace is one of the 750 illustrations in his copy of *Every Man his Own Mechanic*, and inside this book I found a bill for high-class provisions such as Vim. Sometimes we walked down to Cemetery Junction, where we would meet Uncle Fred; we would watch the traffic for a bit then go back for lardy cake and the wrestling on television. After my great grandmother and grandmother both died, Grandad lived on his own until he died in 1974; he had no bathroom and only an outside toilet.

# Emily Gillmor

Boeotian Bell Krater 35.4.5
Two-colour screen print with ink drawing
and Econasign stencil lettering

The Ure Museum is tucked away inside the Department of Classics at the University of Reading. Amongst an array of stunning artefacts, the museum houses one of the largest collections of Greek ceramics in Britain. I am hoping I might inspire more people to discover these rather hidden treasures. My greatest passion is drawing and I am captivated by the beautiful, economical lines used so deftly by Greek ceramicists. Anyone who has tried to draw in a single line will appreciate just how difficult it is! I feel in a way connected to Professor P. N. Ure and his wife Dr A.D. Ure, who established the museum and personally collected the majority of the artefacts on display. My great grandfather, Professor A.W. Seaby, was friends with the Ures and together they shared life at the University in the 1920s. I like to imagine them eagerly discussing a new acquisition – mutually inspiring each other through art and archaeology. Later my father, Robert Gillmor, helped Dr Ure by drawing some Roman coins. I find myself drawn to this elegant bell krater.

URE MUSEUM

# Andrew Boddington

Old Music Rooms, Stained Glass
Coloured glass, glass paint and lead came

The Whiteknights area has been home for me and my family for 35 years, with my children attending the excellent local Redlands School. It is a friendly urban village within Reading, encompassing a thriving community of diverse and creative people due to the proximity of the University, Royal Berkshire Hospital, and schools.

The area's stock of Victorian houses has provided a wonderful opportunity for me to create original stained-glass windows to reinstate what was removed in the mid-20th century. As a glass artist I work with both traditional leaded glass and more modern kiln-fused glass techniques as the project requires.

The Old Music Rooms window was for a front door commission in Upper Redlands Road. The building was originally a private house, was then used by the University of Reading as rooms for the Music Faculty, before once more returning to use as a family home. The present owners wanted a window that would reflect the history of the building while making a bold and colourful statement.

# Pip Hall

In Time
Lino print and ink on paper

I recall the first meeting of the Whiteknights Studio Trail, one late summer's day in 2000. Susanna Beer had returned from travels in New Mexico inspired to start a studio trail in Reading. Meanwhile Jenny was in a process of transforming ideas from her Wargrave Craft Gallery, focusing her energies nearer home. And I, having recently set up my workshop in Marlborough Avenue, was entertaining thoughts of artists' open studios. We each wanted to share with the public our processes, tools and materials as much as to exhibit our work. Through such a convergence of creative, collaborative need, the Trail emerged.

I first worked with Pete Hay (along with Adam Stout) on the inaugural Two Rivers Press book, *Where Two Rivers Meet*. I collaborated on many projects with him subsequently, and still feel his influence strongly in my lettering and lino printing. It felt apt to use this poem of Pete's about the local trees to celebrate the WST anniversary year.

In time
The chestnut tree
has reopened its rooms
for the season
New leaf tiled aisles
decked with candles,
Just in time

# Kennet Quilters

Inspired by Architecture
Patchwork and quilting

A walk around the Studio Trail takes the viewer past a variety of interesting buildings, many falling within Conservation Areas. In particular, the Victorian and Edwardian homes feature embellishments in local bricks, tiles, and glasswork. Modern homes also feature a range of details that can be drawn on for inspiration.

Patchwork often involves the recognition of geometric shapes and their combination into quilts. Likewise, quilting patterns used to hold layers of fabric and wadding together can also be inspired by architecture. Our work here has endeavoured to cover a range of techniques. Tile patterns have influenced the patchwork pieced blocks; architectural chimneys and doorways have been made using fused appliqué techniques; raised tiling has been converted to 'trapunto' quilting, and glasswork has been interpreted in 'stained-glass appliqué'.

# Southern Hill and the area around Whiteknights

1. Christ Church
2. Whitley Villa
3. Hillingdon
4. Abbey School
5. Kensington House
6. Progress Theatre
7. Hillside
8. The Queen's Head
9. Christchurch Green
10. Leighton Park School
11. East Thorpe
12. Elmhurst
13. Broad Oak
14. Redlands School
15. Reading School
16. Alfred Sutton Schools
17. Lakeside Care Home

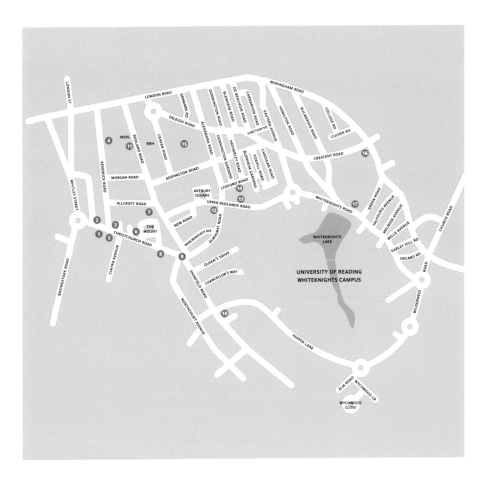

Whitley Pump with Christ Church in the background

Two hundred years ago, the land around the prominent hill to the south of Reading was largely farmland. It had all belonged to the Abbey but, in Tudor times, was distributed amongst the monarch's favoured citizens, the Englefields, the Knollys and the Blagraves. This area was known as Southern Hill and extended from Whitley Street through to what is now Whiteknights Road. The main thoroughfare was, and still is, the road between Reading and Shinfield (Christchurch Road and Shinfield Road). The population growth in the Victorian period, following the move from agriculture to industry and its consequent impact on the town itself, resulted in some significant properties being built, many of which are now protected in three Conservation Areas: Kendrick Road, Christ Church (❶) and The Mount. There are also many Grade II listed buildings and Christ Church itself is Grade II* listed. Until the Reading boundary changes of 1887 this was an area of Whitley that benefited from all the comforts of Reading without any of the cost of being a ratepayer.

The first houses to be built in the 19th century along Southern Hill were Whitley Villa (❷) and the row of terraces that was for a long time known as Whitley Crescent. These were built around 1820 and housed professionals such as schoolteachers and a vicar.

Hillingdon (❸), which has been a hotel for many years, is a brick manufacturer's showreel; a magnificent display of grey, red and moulded brickwork with winged dragons and other finials on the roof. William Poulton, a local brickworks owner, had it built in 1897 and was living there when he was Mayor of Reading (1899–1900). By the mid-1910s the misses Eleanor and Florence Sutton were in residence. During the post-Second World War period, when the house was used by the Milk Marketing Board, it became a film set for The Card, an adaptation of the Arnold Bennett novel, starring Alec Guinness, Petula Clark and Veronica Turleigh.

During the early 19th century, attempts were made by local residents to persuade the parish of St Giles to agree to the erection of a new church to serve the Southern Hill community. In the 1850s the vicar at St Giles finally agreed to a daughter church being built, to be called Christ Church (❶). Henry Woodyer, a local architect, was commissioned to design it, and a chapel-style church without a spire was built on land donated by Sir William Milman. It was consecrated

Cintra Lodge

in 1862. Additional funding was secured and Christ Church became a parish church in its own right. The spire was added in 1874, to a Woodyer design. The original vicarage was built to a design by the renowned architect Alfred Waterhouse in 1871.

Reading High School for Girls was opened on London Road in the 1870s but by the turn of the century had outgrown its buildings. A new school was built and opened in 1905 on Kendrick Road and, after a few years, renamed The Abbey School (❹), reviving the name of the former school in the Abbey Gateway, Forbury Road. A

preparatory school was started in 1905 and, after several moves, a permanent home was provided in 1945 at the present Kensington House (❺) on Christchurch Road on the corner of Vicarage Road. This was originally built as Somerleaze House around 1876 for William Silver Darter, one-time Mayor of Reading, to a design by Alfred Waterhouse.

On the south side of Christchurch Road, the ornate Italian-style Cintra Lodge was the Sutton family home from 1857 until the turn of the 20th century. The name Cintra is thought to come from Sintra in Portugal, famous for its extravagant architecture, and may have been given to the house by an earlier resident, Cajetan Thomas Dias Santos. After Martin Hope Sutton died in 1901, it was used by the Abbey School, the University of Reading and the Ministry of Labour and National Service before being demolished in the 1950s.

Sutherlands, also Italian in style, was built as a home for William Silver Darter on the north side of the road in the 1870s. The name has been retained in a modern house that occupies part of the same plot. Between 1884 and 1888 Arthur Warwick Sutton lived in the house, conveniently close to the much grander Cintra Lodge where he had grown up.

Next to the Sutherlands estate along Christchurch Road is The Mount. This was built in the 1870s, originally for Huntley & Palmers clerks, foremen and managers, and was designed by London architect Robert Austin. A set of stylish houses formed in a square with central terraces, the gault bricks with paler brick banding, as well as the use of Caithness flagstone for kerbs, make the area distinctive.

Between Sutherlands and The Mount is the Progress Theatre (❻). Marianne Faithfull, who was a boarder at St Joseph's Convent (although she lived on nearby Milman Road), joined the theatre when she was about 13 before she went on to enjoy fame alongside the Rolling Stones.

This stretch of Christchurch Road had been an area of piggeries, cow sheds and a beer shop known as the Robin Hood. In 1848 there was a fracas at the pub when William Lunnon of Southern Hill led a mob there carrying sticks, kettles and horns against the landlord. Joseph Patey defended his father Job. Lunnon and his followers fled after a fight. The parties ended up in court after Lunnon sued Patey junior for assault and was bound over to keep the peace.

At the bottom of Lower Mount is Hillside (**7**), the first house erected in Allcroft Road. It was originally built for William Isaac Palmer, the brother of George Palmer, and was completed in 1880 to a design by Morris and Stallwood. After W. I. Palmer died in 1893, the house was acquired by Leonard Sutton and substantially extended by him in 1898. The University of Reading bought the estate in 1949 for student accommodation and it was sold privately in 2013.

The Queen's Head (**8**) dominates the corner of the lane to Whitley Park Farm. The current building dates from the second half of the 19th century but there was a public house on this site before then. The premises have expanded into the building next door, which was the southerly terminus of a Reading Omnibus Company service that ran via the Whitley Pump to West Street.

Approaching Christchurch Green (**9**) there are three late-18th-century Grade II listed properties but sadly the Green at the top of Redlands Road is a mere shadow of what it was then. To the east of the triangle of the Green was the toll gate on the Shinfield Road; to the north were Redlands Road and the town centre. The area

Tennis in front of the Old Dairy by Elmhurst Road

around Redlands Road was depicted in John Speed's map of 1611 with fields, milkmaids and prancing horses. The split into the two parts of the Green that exist today began when Elmhurst Road, originally an extension of Alexandra Road, was laid out to the north. Later the road and the parliamentary boundary ran right through the middle. Nevertheless, together with the parade of shops that was constructed on the south side of Christchurch Road in the early 20th century, this is the spiritual heart of the village.

Venturing from Christchurch Road into Northcourt Avenue, we enter the first road laid out with houses after the sale of the Whitley estate in 1903 following the death of its owner, Samuel Palmer, brother of George. The Avenue was named after the house in London, Northcourt Lodge, in which Samuel had lived.

Heading away from Christchurch Road along Shinfield Road, we find Leighton Park School (❿) by the crossroads at Pepper Lane. In 1889, the Quakers decided to use funds from the sale of their Tottenham-located Grove House School to start Leighton Park School. It was located in a 40-acre park containing a 19th-century house called Pepper Manor, from which the name Pepper Lane came. In 1890, the school for Quaker boys opened and the house was renamed School House. In 1894 a second house was added, Grove House, designed by Alfred Waterhouse, who had family connections to the owners. This allowed the boarding school to grow to 46 boys. Further buildings were added and Cressingham Park, next door, was acquired with its own house.

At the lower end of Redlands Road is the Museum of English Rural Life. The red-brick house next door is East Thorpe (⓫), designed by Alfred Waterhouse in 1879 for Alfred Palmer, son of George Palmer. Alfred Palmer lived here until 1911, when he leased it to the University College (the forerunner of the University of Reading) with a substantial extension for use as a residential hall for female students – St Andrew's Hall. It was extended in 2004 and refurbished to house the Museum, with the University of Reading Special Collections' Archives and Reading Room located in the old Hall.

Near the top of Redlands Road is New Road, a delightful street of varied semi-detached and terraced compact Victorian properties sitting neatly behind garden walls and hedges. A fine stink pipe, lifting the smells from the Victorian sewers above our heads, is situated just as the road turns to the north. It was not until late in the 19th century that one-sided Marlborough Avenue was inserted between New Road and Elmhurst Road.

In 1939, the University of Reading acquired the Elmhurst house and estate (⓬) that had formerly been the home of George Palmer (in the early 1860s) and then of his eldest son, George William Palmer (from 1878 to 1913, when he died). This was on the corner of Upper Redlands Road and Elmhurst Road and the University named it St George's Hall. G. W. Palmer had extended the house to add more rooms and it was further extended by the University, with additional student accommodation blocks built on the estate since 2000. The keystone over the entrance arch to the house bears the initials 'GP' for George Palmer.

Near the corner of Upper Redlands Road and Alexandra Road is Broad Oak (⓭), which was built for Charles Andrewes JP in 1876/7 on land which was originally part of Whiteknights Park. It was bought by the Sutton family after Alderman Andrewes, who was travelling on the bus to the annual meeting of the Corporation when he was taken ill, died in 1895. The house was purchased by Rev. Mother Mary of Calvary in 1909 for the St Joseph's Convent School for girls. Large school buildings were erected for classrooms and other facilities alongside the house and these were completed by 1930.

A little way down the hill, red-brick Redlands School (⓮), founded as Redlands Board School in 1891, sits clinging to the hillside fronting onto Lydford Road. The school was designed by architects Morris and Stallwood.

Reading School (⓯) opened for boys in 1871 on 10 acres acquired from the Redlands Farm estate between Erleigh Road and Addington

Road. It replaced the former school building in Valpy Street that had to close in 1866. The new buildings were designed by Alfred Waterhouse and the foundation stone was laid by the Prince of Wales, later King Edward VII. In 1986, Queen Elizabeth II attended the quincentenary celebrations to mark the date of the charter given by King Henry VII in 1486 after the school's earlier foundation by the monks of Reading Abbey.

The large Mockbeggar estate between Whiteknights Park and Wokingham Road was sold to James Wheble in 1801. Part of the farmland was converted into a brick kiln on land below the Whiteknights Lake, which had been dammed to prevent the stream running down to the river Kennet through the estate. Mockbeggar House, designed by popular local architect Charles Smith, was built in 1866. More of the estate's land was gradually sold off for housing. In 1896, Oliver Dixon, a racehorse trainer, bought the property for riding stables. He and his family lived in the house and continued to own the estate until the 1950s. Berkshire County Council then bought the estate to build the Alfred Sutton Schools (**16**). The house was destroyed by fire in 1999 and was demolished in 2000. The remaining land has since been acquired for the Lakeside Care Home (**17**), after culverting the stream, and by the Ridgeline Trust for therapeutic gardens.

Mockbeggar allotments, the former kitchen gardens of Mockbeggar House, are on a small sloping site next to Lakeside and have been in existence since they were offered for use as part of the Second World War 'Dig for Victory' campaign. Green Road, Talfourd Avenue and other roads off Whiteknights Road also cover parts of the original estate.

*Evelyn Williams & Dennis Wood*

Evelyn Williams is one of the founders of and a regular contributor to the Whitley Pump, a community-based website covering Katesgrove and parts of south Reading. She is actively involved in championing Reading's heritage and is Chair of the Reading Conservation Area Advisory Committee.

Dennis Wood is an author and speaker on the history of Whitley, Southern Hill and surrounding areas. He is Vice Chairman and a Trustee of the Friends of the University of Reading and a tour leader for organised groups visiting the University campuses.

# The Whiteknights Park Estate

## Early history

Records of Earley go back to before the Norman Conquest and feature in the Domesday Book. The Manor of Earley Regis, so named because it was owned by the King, came into the possession of the de Erlegh family in the 12th century. The name Earley Whiteknights was adopted in the early 14th century after John de Erlegh, who was known as the White Knight. A succession of owners followed through the later Middle Ages, notably the Aldryngtons and Bekes, before possession passed to Sir Francis Englefield. When much of the Englefield estates were confiscated for recusancy in 1585, the family moved from Wootton Bassett in Wiltshire to Whiteknights in 1606 to a mansion they built as their substitute home. Although the family remained there for almost 200 years, they gave more attention to literature, religion and science than to beautifying the park. The Marlborough Family Trustees bought the estate in 1798 for George Spencer, the Marquess of Blandford, and his family.

## The Blandford period

The Marquess moved to Whiteknights Park from Bill Hill in nearby Hurst, having previously lived locally at Culham Court in Wargrave. His Grace largely replanned the park and enriched the contents of the mansion – including establishing a lavish library – but in such a profligate manner that he became bankrupt. Having become the 5th Duke of Marlborough in 1817 he withdrew to Blenheim Palace in 1819. The remaining contents of the house and landscape features were sold and the estate returned to descendants of the Englefields. The house was demolished in 1840.

Our knowledge of the development of the park during this period is based largely on *An Account of the Mansion and Gardens of Whiteknights, a Seat of His Grace the Duke of Marlborough*, written in 1819 by Barbara Holland and illustrated with engravings by her husband Thomas Holland. Typically, His Grace failed to pay for their work! Thomas also made two oil paintings of the park which are now owned by the University. The lake was remodelled to its present shape, new paths, tree belts and the road now known as Pepper Lane were laid out, and magnificent gardens were created:

> The *Botanic Gardens* were in the area between the present Park House and Whiteknights House. They contained a grand avenue of elms, rare trees from overseas and formal, variegated and striped gardens. Tropical plants abounded in many glass-houses including an aquarium filled with water lilies.
>
> *The Woods* were located in the area where The Wilderness and the adjoining Harris Garden are today. They contained arcade bowers, an area large enough for His Grace's orchestra, lawns, a vineyard, a rosery and a range of fountains and pavilions. The Grotto, a retreat decorated with seaweeds, minerals and shells, the basic structure of which still survives, was created at the head of the lake and was approached over a rustic bridge.

Georgian gate lodges at Earley Gate

The *New Gardens* were positioned on the north-east perimeter bounded by the current Whiteknights Road and approached from the house over the lake via an iron bridge. They consisted of a series of walkways, borders, groves, rustic timber seats, small arbours and pavilions.

A drive between The Woods and the New Gardens led to the South and North Lodges at the entrance to what is now called Earley Gate. Near the drive was the supposed site of the Chapel of St Nicholas, which was mentioned in the 11th century and where, legend has it,

the White Knight was buried. The Marquess erected a folly on the site, the remains of which were demolished around the turn of the present century.

## The Victorian and Edwardian periods

Several unsuccessful attempts were made to develop the estate in the 1840s before it was purchased in 1849 by Sir Isaac Goldsmid, a member of a family of wealthy London bullion brokers who owned it for the next hundred years. In 1946 it was still owned by a descendant, Sir Henry D'Avignor-Goldsmid, when discussions began for its purchase by the University.

Sir Isaac's initial plan for Whiteknights was as a family home, for which purpose a new house was planned, roughly on the site of the previous mansion. However, the park was instead divided into six leaseholds. The Goldsmids leased the whole estate to Charles Easton, a Reading solicitor, with permission to re-lease it in sections. A house was to be built on each leasehold, which provided an opportunity for an involvement in some of them by the famous architect Alfred Waterhouse. The six leaseholds were:

*Whiteknights Park* (now Park House, though much altered) was built in 1859 by Charles Easton for his own use. It came with 51 acres and three lodges: two within the leasehold and one where its drive (now Chancellor's Way) meets Shinfield Road. In the 1880s it was owned by John Karslake QC.

*Whiteknights* (now Old Whiteknights House), also built in 1859, came with 70 acres, a drive (now Queen's Drive) to Shinfield Road and two lodges. Its grounds included part of Blandford's

Old Whiteknights House

Botanic Gardens. Alfred Waterhouse Senior lived there followed by the local businessman John Heelas.

*Erlegh Park* (or *Erlegh Whiteknights*) was built in 1860 for Thomas Porter III, son of a West Indian plantation owner. Local businessman M Audley Sutton was a later occupant. Its 77 acres of grounds, in the area of the current Wessex Hall, included a lodge by the lake (on Whiteknights Road) and the two Georgian lodges at Earley Gate from the Marquess of Blandford's era.

*The Wilderness* was built in 1865 for Henry Vyse in 59 acres on The Woods area of Blandford's landscape, with lodges on Wilderness Road and the corner of Pepper Lane. Sir Julian Goldsmid MP took the lease in 1872.

*Blandford Lodge* was built in 1867 in 7 acres and was the only leasehold not to include access to the lake. Henry Jago, Captain A. C. Miller and Brigadier-General A. W. Thorneycroft CB were among its early occupants.

*Foxhill* (or *Fox Hill*), built in 1868 by Alfred Waterhouse Junior and lived in by him, was in 28 acres sublet by Alfred Waterhouse Senior from the *Whiteknights* leasehold. The lodge to *Foxhill* on Upper Redlands Road dates from the 1840s when it was built in anticipation of intended developments that failed to materialise. Other well-known occupants included Rufus Isaacs (Marquess of Reading) and Hugo Hirst (Baron Hirst).

A different *Park House* had been built in the 1850s on 7¼ acres of land on Upper Redlands Road in the region of the present Windsor Hall, adjacent to, but not part of, the Whiteknights Park estate. The freehold was also held by the Goldsmids. Captain T. F. Birch RN and local businessmen Edward Jackson JP and M. Audley Sutton were long-term occupants. It was the University's interest in acquiring this property for student accommodation that led to the purchase of the Whiteknights Park estate.

## Whiteknights becomes a university campus

The University of Reading developed from an Extension College of Oxford University in 1892 and became University College Reading in 1902. It moved from Valpy Street to a larger site on London Road in 1905 thanks principally to the generosity of the Palmer and Sutton families and Lady Wantage. Also, land for athletics at Elmhurst Road was made available by George William Palmer and John Heelas. The College was granted university status in 1926 but further development became limited by lack of space.

During discussions about the purchase of Park House on Upper Redlands Road for student accommodation, the University's Bursar had a conversation at a social event with its freeholder, Sir Henry D'Avignor-Goldsmid, who also held the freehold of the neighbouring Whiteknights Park estate. The fortunate outcome was the University's purchase of the freeholds of both Park House in 1946 and the estate in 1947.

Several years of discussion were spent on issues such as the distribution and sequence of the new buildings, what to do with the existing ones, consequences of the existing leaseholds and the future of the London Road site. The estate also suffered from the after-effects of the Second World War, when buildings had been requisitioned and many temporary buildings had been erected.

In consequence, the Victorian buildings were initially used for student accommodation and plans were laid for new academic buildings – to be located together centrally to facilitate interactions – and new halls of residence, to be located in the northern part of the campus. The first building to be constructed was the Faculty of Letters (now the Edith Morley Building), which was formally opened by The Queen in 1957, followed by buildings for Physics and Sedimentology Research in the same architectural style. New buildings in a range of styles continue to be added.

## Earley Gate

During the Second World War a large area of land on the east side of the lake, accessed through the Earley Gate entrance, had been requisitioned and a series of single-storey buildings was erected as a hospital for casualties following the D-Day landings. The buildings were released to the Ministry of Works in 1953 as temporary office buildings (or 'TOBs' as they came to be known) to house many government departments such as Agriculture & Fisheries, Fuel & Power and the Home Office. The area was transferred to the University during 1965–1969 which enabled the departments of Agriculture and Fine Art and Typography to move to Whiteknights from the London Road campus. The TOBs are being progressively replaced by new buildings and only a few remain, including the Reading War Room, now known as 'The Citadel'. This building was constructed by the government during the 1950s as the regional base for Home Defence Region 6 and designed to provide protection from the atomic bomb. When released to the University, the building functioned as a document store until deterioration made it no longer suitable.

## The present

Little of Blandford's gardens remain today although a legacy of fine trees remains, some probably dating from that period. The more tangible survivals are the current boundary of the campus and its areas of open parkland. The remodelled Wilderness contains a range of exotic trees and some garden relics from that time, including the

Grotto, restored in 1985, near which a modern footbridge has replaced the original rustic one. A section of a flint garden wall near Park House also survives from that period.

Though three of the Victorian houses (Park House on Upper Redlands Road, Erlegh Whiteknights and The Wilderness) were demolished in the 1950s and 1960s, largely because of their poor condition, the four that remain (Old Whiteknights House, Park House, Foxhill and Blandford Lodge) still have active roles. Many of the twelve original lodges also remain but a stone arch near Archway Lodge collapsed in 1950.

The acquisition of the Whiteknights Park estate remains the most important single event in the University's history and the natural beauty of the campus is highly valued. Efforts to ensure it is well cared for resulted in Whiteknights receiving its ninth Green Flag award in 2019 as one of Britain's top green spaces.

*Ian Burn & John Grainger*

Ian Burn worked for over 30 years as an administrator in the University Library at Whiteknights. Retirement has allowed him more time to spend pursuing his interest in local history and in particular the history of the University.

John Grainger had an academic career at the University of Reading, where he became Head of the Department of Microbiology. He is a Trustee of the Friends of the University and uses his interest in the history of the University for producing material for Friends' heritage events and other outreach activities.

# Further reading

*A Biographical Dictionary of Architects at Reading* by Sidney M. Gold

*A History of Whiteknights* by Ernest Smith

*A Quiet and Intimate Road* by Adam Sowan (New Road)

*A walk around the Christchurch Conservation Area* by Evelyn Williams, online at www.whitleypump.net

*Conservation Area Appraisals for Christchurch, The Mount and Redlands Conservation Areas.* Reading Borough Council, online at www.readingboroughcouncil/conservationareas

*Earley Days* by Earley Local History Group

*Kerbside Geology in Reading, Berkshire: Aspects of historical archaeology in the expanding town, c.1840–1914* by J. R. L. Allen

*Northcourt Avenue: Its history and its people* by Penny Kemp

*Old Redlands* by Redlands Local History Group

*One Hundred Years of University Education in Reading: A pictorial history 1892–1992* by Dr Sidney Smith and Michael Bott

*Reminiscences of Reading, by an Octogenarian [i.e. William Silver Darter]* by W. S. Darter

*Suttons Seeds: A history 1806–2006* by Earley Local History Group

*Views from the Hill: The story of Whitley* by Dennis Wood

Two Rivers Press has been publishing in and about Reading
since 1994. Founded by the artist Peter Hay (1951–2003), the press
continues to delight readers, local and further afield, with its varied list
of individually designed, thought-provoking books.